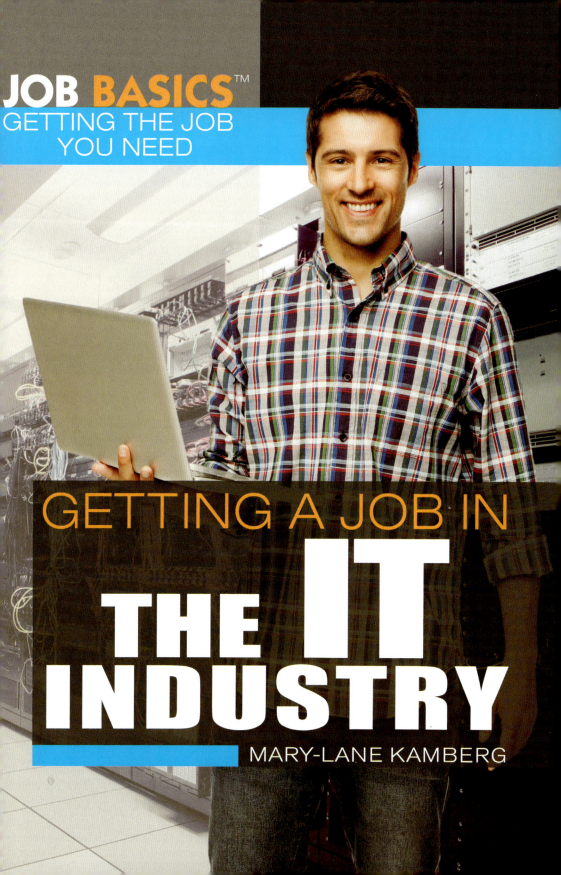

For Rebekka Rohrback

Published in 2017 by The Rosen Publishing Group
29 East 21st Street, New York, NY 10010

Copyright 2017 by The Rosen Publishing Group, Inc.

First Edition

All rights reserved. No part of this book may be reproduced in any form without permission in writing from the publisher, except by a reviewer.

Library of Congress Cataloging-in-Publication Data

Names: Kamberg, Mary-Lane, 1948- author.
Title: Getting a job in the IT industry / Mary-Lane Kamberg.
Other titles: Job basics, getting the job you need.
Description: First edition. | New York : Rosen Publishing, 2017. | "2017 | Series: Job basics: getting the job you need | Audience: Grades 7 to 12. | Includes bibliographical references and index.
Identifiers: LCCN 2016006634 | ISBN 9781477785560 (library bound)
Subjects: LCSH: Information technology—Vocational guidance—Juvenile literature. | Computer science—Vocational guidance—Juvenile literature. | Vocational guidance.
Classification: LCC T58.5 .K35 2017 | DDC 004.023—dc23
LC record available at http://lccn.loc.gov/2016006634

Manufactured in China

CONTENTS

	INTRODUCTION	4
Chapter One	WHAT'S IT ALL ABOUT?	7
Chapter Two	LAYING THE GROUNDWORK	16
Chapter Three	SELLING YOURSELF: BUILDING A RESUME	27
Chapter Four	ON THE (JOB) HUNT	38
Chapter Five	INTERVIEWING FOR IT	49
Chapter Six	THE FIRST DAY AND BEYOND	59
	GLOSSARY	66
	FOR MORE INFORMATION	68
	FOR FURTHER READING	71
	BIBLIOGRAPHY	73
	INDEX	77

INTRODUCTION

Each week, the accounting team at XYZ Company receives an e-mail from the sales team about the week's sales. A clerk copies and pastes the information into a spreadsheet. He or she then calculates each sales representative's commission based on a percentage of sales. The clerk e-mails the amount that each salesperson earned to the payroll department. There, another employee enters the amounts into the payroll system. Checks are then issued to each member of the sales force.

This manual task takes time and repeats every week. Company officials wonder whether using computer technology for these tasks could save time. Could it save money? Could it reduce human error? These are the things that information technology (IT) has been developed to address.

The company asks the IT team (or outsources the job) to write an application. An application is a software program with a specific use. In this case, the application will be designed to take in the sales numbers, calculate the commissions, and send them directly into the payroll system. The computer can even spit out a report that an accounting person can double-check for accuracy. Using the computer program helps the company run more efficiently and with greater accuracy than the human method. It also frees the accounting team for other tasks. It might also mean that the employer can reduce its staff and payroll.

Computer system design and related service industries are a vital part of modern business. Their importance creates a high demand for employees. Businesses need workers who can create software, maintain networks, ensure electronic security, and perform computer design and other services.

According to the U.S. Department of Labor, information technology jobs will grow by 12 percent between 2014 and

Information technology helps businesses save time and run efficiently. Workers in this field will be in demand over the next decade.

2024. That rate is faster than the average for all jobs. The IT field is expected to add about 488,500 new jobs, from about 3.9 million jobs to about 4.4 million jobs, during the same period.

The IT industry includes such workers as developers/programmers, computer systems analysts, information security analysts, database administrators, network and computer system administrators, computer or network architects, computer support specialists, and computer research scientists. Whatever your interests and skills, the field of information technology likely has a place for you.

All you need is training and experience to qualify for the job you want. High school classes can build a foundation. Post-secondary school choices include certificate programs, associate's degree programs, and bachelor's degree programs. This education is available through community colleges, as well as four-year and career colleges and universities. You can attend traditional on-campus classes. Online learning is also easy to find. Finally, internships can give you the experience that companies and IT firms are looking for. An internship is a temporary work experience that offers on-the-job training.

Does an IT career sound like something you'd be interested in? Read on to learn more about how to join this growing and essential career field.

CHAPTER ONE
What's IT All About?

The IT industry includes a wide range of computer-related jobs. For example, when changing a manual commission system to a computer-based, one often starts by consulting with a systems analyst. A systems analyst reviews the way the company uses technology. He or she will determine if there is a more efficient way to perform a task. In this instance, a computer program can replace e-mail and Microsoft Excel spreadsheets created by the accounting department.

Next, a software developer/programmer will be needed. Software developers use the analysis of user needs and add their own creativity to design general software or customized programs that help clients improve efficiency. Developers may also analyze and design databases. Or, they might develop systems for computers or other devices or networks.

A software developer at XYZ company will make this new application. Let's call it the Commission Calculator. Maybe you work "in house" for the company itself, or maybe you work for a software company that XYZ company hires. Software companies create programs and then sell or license them to other companies.

Some developers work for businesses, but many work for computer system design firms or software publishers. Software developers usually have a bachelor's degree in

GETTING A JOB IN **THE IT INDUSTRY**

computer science. They also have strong computer programming skills.

Get With the Program

Developers may supervise programmers. Programmers tell the computer what to do. They write and test codes that make applications work. Computer code is an arrangement of instructions to a computer. Coders use letters and numbers represented as binary numbers. The binary number

Video game developers and programmers need advanced technical training so they can write code and design games. Some universities and art institutes provide coursework in game design and development.

system, also known as Base 2, represents numeric values using only the digits zero and one. Simply, zero turns off the electronic circuit voltage. One turns it on.

Using different programming languages, programmers take designs created by software developers and engineers and convert them into computer instructions. Programmers usually work in offices in the systems design industry. Most programmers have a bachelor's degree, but some start with an associate's degree.

One type of developer/programmer is known as a Web developer. A Web developer performs the same kinds of tasks as other developers and programmers. The difference is their work appears on the Internet. For example, someone may develop software and write code for online banking or create a company's website.

Another difference is that a website developer or webmaster typically creates content. This task is unique to web development. In addition to computer skills, these developers need such skills as writing and graphic design. Web developers start their careers with a high school diploma. However, most need at least an associate's degree.

Database Admins

Once XYZ Company has the software for its Commission Calculator, database administrators will store the input and output data. Input is the data entered into a computer. Output is the result after the program performs its tasks.

In this case, the data input includes sales figures. The output includes the amounts of pay. In other cases, the data may include financial information or customer shipping records. In many cases, the data may be sent to long-term storage.

LET'S PLAY

If you're a video game fan—or gamer—you may sometimes dream about creating your own games. Game developers or programmers usually pick this particular part of the industry to work in because they love video games with a passion. They need good problem-solving skills. And they must work quickly under pressure. As with all jobs, they need training and experience.

Amateurs can make their own games using software packages without having to write code. Software exists for 3-D, 2-D, and role-playing games. Examples include DarkBASIC, DarkBASIC Pro, Game Maker, Game Editor, RPG Toolkit, Hephaestus, Mugen, Adventure Game Studios (AGS), and others. Experience using this kind of software may be helpful in getting hired by a game company.

But, this field is competitive. If you want to invent games as a career, you need advanced technical training. The ability to write code is an important skill. Software code programs to know include C++, Python, Visual Basic, and Perl.

In addition, many online and on-campus schools offer degrees in this field. For example, Full Sail University, DeVry University, and many art institutes offer individual courses as well as bachelor's degree programs in game art, game design, game development, and game programming.

Qualifications for database administrators usually include a bachelor's degree in database management, computer science information systems, or information technology. Applicants also need an understanding of database languages. Work experience is preferred.

At XYZ Company, other administrators—network and computer system administrators—will install the Commission Calculator onto the physical machine where it will run. They will hook up the cables that ensure the Commission Calculator can connect with the company's payroll system. This

WHAT'S IT ALL ABOUT?

connection is known as an interface. An interface is computer hardware or software that communicates with other devices and/or programs.

Making Plans

A computer system includes computers that are connected and share a central storage system. It also includes such

Businesses that use information technology rely on computer hardware to work properly. They need workers to operate and maintain their machines and computer devices.

hardware devices as printers, scanners, or routers. A computer network is a group of computer systems and other hardware devices. Network and computer systems administrators are responsible for the day-to-day operation of these physical computer devices.

Some IT assignments are more complicated than XYZ's Commission Calculator. For these, a computer network architect helps determine and recommend the needed hardware and network architecture. Computer architecture is a plan that shows how software and hardware technology work together to form a computer system.

Computer network architects recommend the overall strategy. Next, they design and build the system. Examples of their work include such data communication networks as local area networks (LANs) and wide area networks (WANs). The networks may simply connect two or more

UNDERSTANDING LINGO AND JARGON

Job titles in the IT field indicate the level of the individual's skills and responsibilities. Look for the last word of the title. The following words are in order from the lowest level of qualifications and responsibilities to the highest.

Specialist – computer support specialist, help desk specialist

Administrator – database administrator, network administrator, or computer systems administrator

Engineer – computer software engineer and computer hardware engineer

Architect – network architect, computer architect

Computer research scientist

offices. Or, they may include cloud infrastructure for large numbers of users.

A computer network architect might collaborate with the developer while an application is still being created. In turn, a network administrator might perform more basic work. Examples include installing applications and making maintenance upgrades to servers and other hardware. Qualifications for IT architects usually include a bachelor's degree in computer science, information systems, or engineering and a master's of business administration in information systems.

Other Jobs

Once an application is ready to go, a computer support specialist will learn about it. Computer support specialists are often called "help desk" representatives. They are the ones who take the system back to the users. In this case, users include: 1) the sales team who will be entering the data (sales numbers) into the system, 2) the payroll employees, who will now perform tasks in a new way, and 3) accounting personnel, who will now get a report rather than monthly numbers.

Computer support specialists are also the ones who get calls when something goes wrong. They know the troubleshooting steps to use when something crashes or data seems wrong. They answer the calls and help the users—even months or years down the road.

Applicants for a help desk position need a high school diploma plus some post-secondary education in the field.

Two more jobs in the IT industry include information security analysts and computer research scientists. Information security analysts are responsible for keeping applications

GETTING A JOB IN **THE IT INDUSTRY**

from being "hacked." They work closely with network architects and administrators to ensure the safety of all applications in an organization's network, including XYZ Company's Commission Calculator. These workers need a bachelor's degree in information security, computer science, or

A job as a help desk specialist is a good way to begin an IT career. These employees help co-workers and customers understand new applications and troubleshoot problems.

programming and (often) a master's of business administration (MBA) in information systems.

Finally, computer research scientists are the smartest of the smart in the IT industry. They worry less about how to use technology to improve business efficiency and more about designing the technology in the first place. Rather than thinking about how to move banking onto the Internet, they invented the Internet in the first place. They deal with big concepts and how to make them happen.

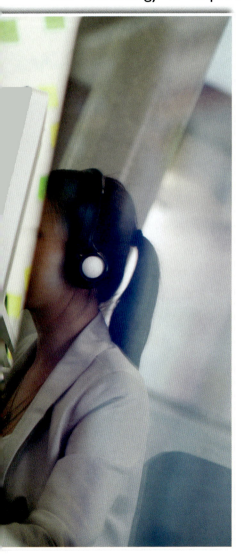

Computer research scientists need a doctoral degree. They may work for computer system design services, colleges or professional schools, software publishers, or in businesses' research and development departments. Or, they may be involved in independent research.

Typical pay ranges for all IT jobs vary according to the position and the employee's training and experience. For current information about the median annual wage for computer and information technology occupations in the United States, visit the U.S. Department of Labor's Bureau of Labor Statistics online.

CHAPTER TWO

Laying the Groundwork

IT is not a one-size-fits-all sector. What kinds of education, training, and work experience do you need for the IT job you want? To find out, visit government and job websites. For example *The Occupational Outlook Handbook* published by the U.S. Department of Labor's Bureau of Labor Statistics gives information on job descriptions, qualifications, salary ranges, and outlook for future jobs.

You can also search Internet job sites to see which education and technical skills employers are looking for. Most listings are very specific about the experience and necessary languages and expertise each position requires.

Starting Early

If you're interested in a career in the IT industry, start learning as soon as you have access to a computer. Learn to use such basics as Microsoft Office, Windows, Mac, and other program packages and operating systems. Many high school classes can increase your comfort level in various areas of interest. Some secondary schools offer such computer studies classes as an overview of the industry, graphic and web design, information technology, and programming.

LAYING THE GROUNDWORK

Many high schools offer classes that cover basic through advanced computer skills to help prepare students for living in the 21st Century, as well as for careers in information technology.

For example, When Olathe Northwest High School opened in Olathe, Kansas, in 2003, it was designed as a school for the twenty-first century. Each student got a Personal Digital Assistant (PDA). Technology replaced handwritten assignments. The curriculum covered such advanced database skills as data mining, analysis, manipulation, and warehousing. It also included how to build real-world computer and software engineering applications. These applications served the school and community. Finally, it developed computer and server programming skills through project-based learning.

This school was a forerunner in a movement of tech-focused high schools out there. Classes offered included a wide variety of subject matter, including e-communication, graphic design, web design, web development, video production, and animation, along with general education courses like English, history, mathematics, and science. Similar schools may also offer classes in such programming languages as Java, C++, and Advanced C++. You'll also benefit from developing communication skills (both written and verbal) by taking classes

Learning such programming languages as Java (pictured here), C++, and Advanced C++ helps prepare students both to use those languages and adapt to new ones in the future.

in speech, writing, and art (especially for a career in Web design).

Business classes teach the basic operations of companies, why they are important, and how they work together. Look for overview business classes and classes in accounting, personal finance, and financial management.

Beyond High School

Some entry-level jobs in the IT industry, such as software testers, website developers, and some help desk specialists, require only a high school diploma. However, most IT jobs require a bachelor's degree plus years of experience. If you want a lifelong IT career, you'll likely need additional post-secondary work from specialized technical training courses, community colleges, or career or traditional colleges and universities. Many of these institutions offer night classes or online study, which is convenient, especially if you have a job or other obligations.

Choose Carefully

Be careful when choosing a school. Investigate the school's program, as well as its cost and the kind of job placement success their graduates have had. Ask whether the school arranges work-study or internships and how successful graduates have been in landing a job. Also find out whether credit for coursework at the school will transfer to other institutions. This is especially important if you may want to pursue higher level degrees in the future.

GETTING A JOB IN **THE IT INDUSTRY**

The Ray and Maria Stata Center, known as "The Stata," houses the computer science department and laboratory on the campus of the Massachusetts Institute of Technology in Cambridge, Massachusetts.

Some IT training schools, including programs at larger technical or private colleges, have negative reputations. Schools that provide substandard training and weak job placement, despite promising otherwise, are sometimes known as diploma mills. A certificate or degree from them won't help—and might hurt—your ability to land a job.

Before enrolling, be sure the school is accredited by an organization recognized by the U.S. Department of Education (USDE) or the Council of Higher Education Accreditation (CHEA). Accreditation is a voluntary review by a non-government agency. The agency sets standards of educational quality and determines whether a school meets them. The goal of these organizations is to hold institutions accountable and ensure that their programs actually help students qualify for jobs in their fields of study.

In the United States, the Accreditation Board for Engineering and Technology (ABET) is the best known accrediting agency for IT-related degree programs. ABET accreditation ensures that credits transfer to other educational institutions, as well as be recognized by employers in the field. ABET is recognized by the U.S. Department of Education. Websites for ABET, USDE, and CHEA post current lists of accrediting agencies, schools, and programs.

Getting Started

Accreditation is especially important for programs that offer information technology certificates. Research the schools that offer these certificates, avoiding scams and diploma mills. Otherwise, you'll waste time and money for a useless piece of paper.

GETTING A JOB IN **THE IT INDUSTRY**

Students learn how computers work by programming a Raspberry Pi, a credit card-sized device that plugs into other computer hardware.

Legitimate information technology certificates are available at the college undergraduate and graduate levels. Undergraduate certification shows that the student has basic skills in computer systems, networks, and programming.

Basic certificate programs are geared toward those with little IT background. Higher level graduate certificates for experienced IT professionals come from advanced training in specific areas. In addition, such computer related hardware or software firms as Microsoft and Cisco offer advanced certification programs to enhance IT professionals' expertise in their products.

Enrollment qualifications depend on the level of certification pursued, but students need at least a high school diploma. Basic undergraduate certification requires five to twelve classes over one to two years. Depending on their work experience, certificate holders may be ready for such entry level jobs as help desk, systems administrator, or network administrator. However, many employers prefer to hire applicants with associate's degrees plus professional experience, or candidates with bachelor's degrees

Major Considerations

College and university students can choose from five major areas of study for bachelor's degrees in IT. Computer engineering involves designing and building or inventing such items as silicon chips, smartphones, and other computerized devices. Computer science majors are problem solvers with good math skills. They learn to design such products as search engines and operating systems.

A third area of study is software engineering. This subject may be part of a computer science major, but in some schools it's its own degree. The fourth area is called information systems. This major includes both business and technology topics. It focuses on how computers make companies more effective. Information systems may also be known as management information systems, computer information systems, or business information systems.

The final field of study is known as information technology. This name can be confusing, because many people group all computer technologies under that title. However, a major in information technology focuses on both the hardware and software that supports an organization. Students learn how to select computer systems, design company websites, and troubleshoot.

Traditional community colleges, as well as four-year colleges and universities, offer these fields of study. They lead to associate's, bachelor's, and post-graduate degrees. So do career colleges and universities like University of Phoenix, ITT Technical Institute, and DeVry University. These technical schools have many campuses across the country and offer career-focused programs. They offer both on-campus and online classes that include general education courses like English, social studies, humanities, and math.

Sign Me Up

To apply for a certificate or degree program, visit the school's website. Check for enrollment requirements. Pay attention to deadlines for application. Most schools offer online applications with easy-to-follow steps.

If you need financial assistance, first fill out the Free Application for Federal Student Aid (FAFSA). Your application will be used by institutions of higher learning to determine

TIPS FOR ONLINE LEARNING SUCCESS

If you're thinking about taking an online IT course, you may not know much about this type of learning. Online classes often are more convenient than campus classes, but they are not easier.

- You'll have to demonstrate the same academic dedication as in other schools. Success depends on motivation, self-discipline, and time management. These tips will help you make the most of this opportunity.
- Become familiar with the school's expectations, and complete your assignments on time.
- Arrange for reliable Internet access. Be sure to save and backup your work frequently. Use cloud storage like Dropbox so you can work from your smart phone or tablet. Save instructors' contact information in multple places.
- Create a study schedule and calendar to track test dates and assignment deadlines. Give yourself time to complete tasks without last-minute cramming or panic. Stick to your schedule.
- Use lists and time limits. Estimate how long assignments take. On Mondays, list what you must complete by the end of the week.
- Build a relationship with instructors, and ask for help.
- Review your work and notes to keep them fresh in your mind. When exam time comes, you'll find studying easy.
- Participate. Some courses require online discussions. Even if yours doesn't, use social media to connect with your virtual classmates. You can also ask them for help understanding concepts or assignments.

whether you qualify for financial aid—and how much you qualify for. The government sends a copy of this form to the school(s) you apply to. You may also have to fill out a financial aid application at the school you plan to attend.

You may be offered financial aid in the form of grants, loans, or campus employment. Before signing anything, ask your high school guidance counselor or other independent professional for help. He or she can check out the numbers and explain such terms of repayment as length of time, amount of payments, and any penalties for early payment or nonpayment.

Online classes are convenient, but not necessarily easier than in-person instruction. Student success depends on motivation and time-management skills, as well as staying on schedule.

CHAPTER THREE

Selling Yourself: Building a Resume

When employers have jobs to fill, they want to hire the best candidates. Your job is to convince them that you fit the bill. A resume is your first chance to show them. It tells them who you are.

A résumé is a document that summarizes your education and personal and professional experience. Its job is to get you an interview. It's often your only chance to make that important first impression. A resume must present you in the best possible light. It must also be true and accurate. And each item on it should help show the employer why you're the best person for the job.

You should craft a different resume for each position you apply for, even if you only tweak each one slightly. Each resume must be tailored to the job opening. Use the information you learned by visiting the employer's website and reading its media releases. Identify its major issues and emphasize the ways your qualifications make you the best candidate to help the employer solve them. If you have solved similar problems elsewhere, lead off with that experience. If not, show how your education and experience gave you the skills needed to do that.

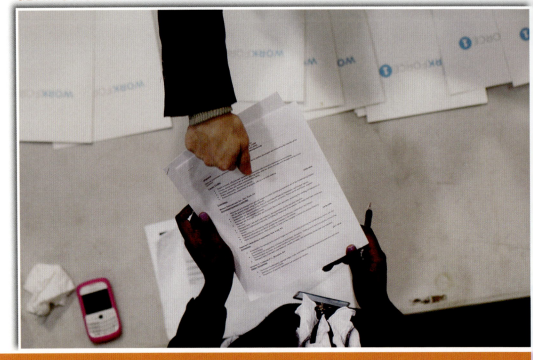

The goal of a resume is to get you an employment interview. It should be neat and attractive, as well as true and accurate, without too much technical jargon, beyond listing your credentials using or developing software and hardware.

It's Elementary

In addition to being tailored to a specific job, a good resume contains important elements. It should stress specific accomplishments, not responsibilities. Whenever possible, use numerical or percentage results to quantify your results. Many job seekers simply list what they did at a previous job. For example, if you worked at XYZ Company, you might say something like "wrote code for new applications." Instead, a better way to frame that experience would be "wrote code for XYZ Company's Commission Calculator, which reduced the company's operational costs by twelve percent."

Another important part of a resume is its appearance. It should be neat and unassuming in terms of normal fonts and white space. This is no time to show your creativity with strange typefaces or quirky layouts. Use Times New Roman or Arial font in a 10-point or 12-point size. Avoid a crammed-in look. Aim for a border of 1 inch (2.54 centimeters) on all four sides of the page. Double-check grammar and spelling visually and using your spell-check and grammar check on your word processor. Utilize the same style throughout the document. For instance, if you use bullet points in one section, don't switch to dashes in another. The same goes for using bold, italics, or underlining.

Finally, the resume should be easy for a "civilian" to read. The human relations department employee who selects applicants for interviews may not have the same training as you or your potential boss. Avoid overuse of industry jargon that only techies understand.

Organize, Then Organize Some More

IT employers look for education, experience, and technical skills. The way you organize your resume depends on what you have to offer. You'll want to include an education section and a work experience section that lists key accomplishments. If you have technical skills and/or project experience, add a section for each.

Many books on writing resumes suggest that you add a section about your objectives in the new job. However, since IT jobs are so varied, and you may qualify for more than one opening, an objective may actually work to your disadvantage. Leave it out, and let your skills and experience speak for themselves.

JOHN SMITH
(555) 987-6543 · E-mail: johnsmith@abc.com

EDUCATION

UNIVERSITY, City, State   **MMM YYYY – MMM YYYY**

Bachelor of Science in Management Information Systems

- Graduated with Honors, Cumulative 3.38 on 4.0 scale
- Coursework in application development, network architecture, database management systems, and the role of technology in organizations

JUNIOR COLLEGE, City, State   **MMM YYYY – MMM YYYY**

- Coursework in Science, English Literature, and Composition

PROJECTS

Create an algorithm to process academic research data   **MMM YYYY – present**

Advisor: Professor Pranav Patel
- Goal: create a scalable algorithm to process student questionnaire responses for a graduate program research project
- Coded in Java to read from text files, calculate percentages and perform other analysis of the data, and store the information to a database
- Utilized variables, assignment statements, arithmetic expressions, input and output statements
- Team leader among four-student team: responsible for planning, assigning tasks, communicating with advisor, and proofreading the team's official project document

Design a mobile application   **MMM YYYY – MMM YYYY**

Advisors: Professor David Johnson; Ms. Mary Jones, owner, Campus Outfitters Camping Store
- Semester-long project partnering college students with a local campus store that sells camping gear
- Students collaborated to create a functional mobile application focusing on a user-friendly interface and the ability to link to common online payment capabilities (e.g. PayPal)
- Earned an A, 94 of 100 points possible. Site has processed more than 1,500 orders since going live

INTERNSHIPS

COMPANY NAME, INC. City, State   **MMM YYYY – MMM YYYY**

<Company Name> is a regional telecommunications equipment and services company headquartered in City, State. It is the fourth-largest mobile service provider in the region by subscriber base.

- Learned basic mobile device and networking design concepts
- Assisted the frontline workers to identify and correct SIM card defects
- Invited by the intern program manager to return the following summer

GENERAL WORK EXPERIENCE

Joe's Shake Shack City, State   MMM YYYY – MMM YYYY

- Worked as a line cook and server for three summers during high school and college
- Demonstrated punctuality; developed communication and leadership skills

ACTIVITIES AND HONORS

President, Danville High School Student Association   MMM YYYY – MMM YYYY

- Led daily operations and planned annual activities
- Recruited 24 new members
- Organized three school-wide activities to enrich school spirit, with 120 participants in total

Outstanding Student Cadre Award

- Won the YYYY Student Council's award for Outstanding Student Cadre during term as student association president

VOLUNTEERING

Painter, Habitat for Humanity, City, State   MMM YYYY

- Led the painting team consisting of 11 students and adults
- Organized supplies and developed a plan to complete exterior paint for 3 homes in a single day
- Coordinated with the Habitat forewoman and communicated to the team

SUMMARY OF TECHNICAL EXPOSURE

Proficiency with JavaScript applications and Java applets • Java/C++ on SUSE Linux • Java on Redhat Linux • Microsoft Word • Microsoft PowerPoint • *Exposure to* Java on Sun Solaris Unix • Microsoft Excel

---

This sample resume is a good example of one for a recent graduate with little work experience. It emphasizes his education and technical skills. It also gives employers a good idea of his leadership potential. Because he was president of his high school student association and won an important award, these items are listed. However, no other high school activities are relevant, and so they are omitted

Structure the resume according to your situation. If you're still attending a post-secondary school or you're a recent graduate without work experience—or without much work experience—list education first. Otherwise, move education to the end of the document.

In the education section, list your major and minor (if any), your grade point average (GPA), related courses (for example, business courses), activities, and awards. List only IT-related activities in this section. President of the computer club counts. Playing on the intramural rugby team does not. (Unless, of course, you know that your interviewer played rugby!) If there are experiences or activities that will help you connect with your interviewer, add them.

Omit high school information, unless the interviewer has a connection to your school or you achieved something exceptional there.

First Things First

At the top of your resume put your name, phone number, e-mail address, and personal website if you have one and it looks professional. Ensure that your e-mail address does not appear unprofessional. If yours is anything like partyguy@abc.com, create a new e-mail account using just your name for the purpose of job hunting. (Also be sure your social media reflects only professional attitudes and lifestyles. Many employers will do basic searches of social media websites to identify potential concerns about a candidate. So it's a good idea to review your own publicly available information. Edit the Spring Break or weekend party photos to ensure you present a professional image.)

SELLING YOURSELF: BUILDING A RESUME

Most IT employers first want to know about a candidate's work experience. So create sections for your work experience and IT related internships. List your most recent employment first in reverse chronological order.

Be brief. You don't need to include every job you ever had. The last three to five places of employment are plenty. List only jobs with relevant experience. Omit working at McDonald's or your uncle's lawn service business. However, if you have no previous IT experience, listing other jobs can show such traits as dedication, maturity, and

If you have work experience in the field, list it first. Otherwise, list your education and any special training. Listing experience in computer-related electronics retail is perfectly acceptable for entry-level IT applicants.

GETTING A JOB IN **THE IT INDUSTRY**

Many hobbies can help your future IT career, such as partaking in the Maker Movement, whose participants build and repair simple electronics. Others teach themselves how to take apart and put back together computer hardware.

SELLING YOURSELF: BUILDING A RESUME

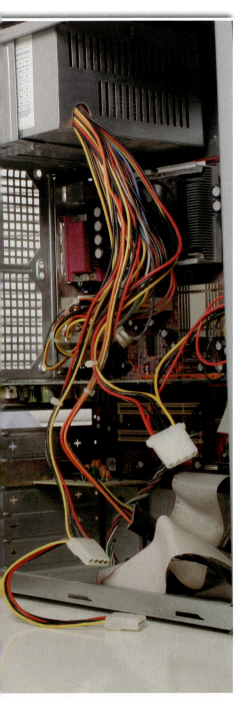

punctuality. For non-IT jobs, emphasize skills you learned that will contribute to an IT job.

If you have no internships or work experience, make a section near the end of the resume for life experiences that translate to job skills. Are you bilingual? List the languages you are fluent or conversational in. Being a club officer shows leadership. List a project you chaired like a homecoming float you designed or a soccer tournament you organized. These activities show that you can make things happen.

If you do have work experience, pay attention to the kinds of things that jump off the page for your interviewer. Most people list their previous job titles, employer, and dates worked. However, if you worked for such leading IT companies as Microsoft, Intel, Cisco or others, put the employer's name first (in bold type).

Your resume should include a section with a list of projects you've worked on, along with

35

key accomplishments. This section of the resume should follow your list of past employment. Or, if none, place it just after your education information. Focus on your achievements related to the projects.

Employers in the IT industry also are interested in the technical skills you possess. Make a separate section to list software, programming languages, foreign languages, or other skills you have. Omit such skills as familiarity with Microsoft Office and Windows. The employer will assume you have at least that level of competence.

Your resume might have all of these sections or only some of them. And you might want to arrange them in a different order. Remember, the purpose of the resume is to give a sense of who you are and get an interview. Don't be afraid to go "off-script" a little bit. Let your resume reflect your unique qualities, skills, and experiences.

What to Include, and What to Leave Out

When you send your resume, send copies of any certifications you have earned, such as special training in a particular type of software. You don't need copies of associate's or bachelor's degrees. The employer will get them from your school.

Some information should not appear on a resume. One is your list of references. They should appear on a separate sheet of paper. Only offer the list if the recruiter requests it. References should ideally be people you have had meaningful interactions with, but generally not former employers. Always be sure to ask permission to list them.

SELLING YOURSELF: BUILDING A RESUME

Other experience that may be helpful, even it is unpaid, is volunteering as a computer lab assistant in school. Make sure to think hard about all the experience you have and whether it should go on your resume.

In both the United States and Canada, recruiters must be careful about potential discrimination claims. They don't want to see information about your race, religion, gender, sexual preference, or whether you're married or have children on your resume. And never include your photograph, which reveals your race and gender. There should be no reason any employer would ask for such information. If they do, they risk being reported and incurring legal penalties.

Finally, for some jobs, make your resume scannable. Use ASCII Text formatting. Use a 12-point or 14-point size of a simple font. Use only tabs and spaces. Avoid borders, columns, underlines, bold face, and italics. Send it in the body of an e-mail and as an attachment.

CHAPTER FOUR

On the (Job) Hunt

If you don't have a job, your job is to hunt for one. That means, ideally, spending roughly eight hours a day (a normal work day) looking for one. You don't have to go it alone, though. Many workers in all fields get jobs through personal contacts. Reach out to teachers, advisors, neighbors, friends, and friends' parents. Tell everyone you are looking for a job in information technology. Ask if anyone knows someone in the IT industry. Ask them to help you connect with someone in the business.

Try to find an IT worker—or several—to talk to as part of an "information interview." An information interview is a conversation with a professional to learn about the field and local job market. Ask for an appointment for a fifteen- or twenty-minute interview.

Make a list of questions to ask. Some typical questions include:

- How did you become an IT professional?
- What do like best and least about the job?
- What tips do you have for someone starting out?
- What is the range of salaries in the community?
- Do you know of any jobs right now?

If you conduct the interview in person, arrive on time. Stay only as long as the agreed limit. The same goes for an interview

ON THE (JOB) HUNT

During your job search, seek out an IT professional who will meet you for an information interview about the industry. Ask for help connecting with potential employers.

you conduct by telephone. Afterward, thank the interviewee. Leave your name and contact information in case he or she later learns of a job opening you might be a good fit for.

Send a thank you e-mail or handwritten thank you note. From time to time, drop the professional a note or e-mail to stay in touch. When you land a job, let him or her know where you are working and again give thanks for the help.

GETTING A JOB IN **THE IT INDUSTRY**

Join professional organizations and start building a network of others involved in the IT sector. Benefits include opportunities for employment networking, informal learning, and even simply making friends who share your interests.

ON THE (JOB) HUNT

Join the Club

Professional organizations are good places to meet others who work in IT. For example, the Association of Information Technology Professionals has local chapters to help members advance their careers. Its programs and activities include members-only webinars and conferences, a career center, and the ability to network with others at local meetings and online. Its newsletter keeps members up-to-date on industry trends.

Two professional groups where women and African Americans can network with others and find opportunities for professional development are the Association for Women in Computing and Black Data Processing Associates (BDPA). AWC is a non-profit organization of female professionals working in or having interest in the Computer Science and Information Technology Fields.

AWC promotes advancement of women in the computing professions. It offers programs on technical and career topics. BDPA does the same for male and female African Americans.

Look for IT organizations with local chapters that you can join. They are great places to build your professional network. Through other members, you can learn about available positions in the industry now and in the future.

Get Social

Social networking is getting more and more important in making connections that lead to present (or future) jobs. Take advantage of the Internet to create a presence in the industry. That will help you connect to the hidden job market. The hidden job market refers to jobs that are not posted or advertised, but rather filled through personal connections. Build a network of connections through social websites.

For instance, search social networking sites by job title, company name, or ZIP code. You'll find profiles of individuals you might want to contact through those you know. Or, you might find a common interest in a group you both belong to.

The best networking site for this kind of search is LinkedIn, but other sites work in similar ways. Google+ offers similar services and advantages. Joining one—or both—gives you a chance to develop professional connections. It also gives you a chance to be noticed by employers.

Boot Up

Start by creating a profile. You need a photo of yourself. (Although photos don't belong on resumes, they're perfectly fine on social media.) Take the time to get a professional headshot. It doesn't have to be expensive. Such retailers as Target, Walmart, and J.C. Penney have photo departments with reasonable prices. With the quality of smartphones today, you can even get a friend (preferably a pro or amateur photographer) to take a decent one.

The next important item is your headline. A social networking headline is a mini resume. It tells who you are and what you do. Before writing your own, take a look at other headlines on the network to see what others have done. Be sure to include keywords for your skills, as well as the job title you're interested in. These are the elements that will pop up when a potential employer searches the site. The rest of the sections on these sites let you post your training, education, and work experience. And you can simply link to your full resume.

Finally, Twitter gives you ways to follow companies you're interested in, as well as ways to expand your presence on the Web. For Twitter, keep your handle professional. The same goes for your hashtags. A hashtag is a word or phrase that follows a hash mark (#). It makes it easy for those searching for the topic or keyword of your tweet. Avoid such hashtags as "unemployed" or "needajob." Instead, use such words or phrases as:

- #resume
- #linkedin
- #software programmer
- #website developer
- #database administrator

GETTING A JOB IN **THE IT INDUSTRY**

Twitter can be your new best friend when you're looking for a job. Be sure to use professional hashtags that drive the Twitterverse to you and your tweets.

Twitter is a good place to learn about job openings. Follow IT employers in your area and watch for tweets about opportunities. Search for hashtags that employers use:

- #hiring
- #joblisting
- #jobopening
- #jobpostings
- #opportunity

You can also use Twitter apps to keep track of openings. Try TwitJobSearch, TweetMyJobs, JobShouts, and MicroJobs.

Once your profiles are in place, build your networks. Contact past employers, schoolmates, neighbors, and friends, as well as those you know from professional organizations or special interest groups. Then start posting professional information. For example, comment on an article in a respected newspaper or magazine about the IT industry. Provide a link to it. Keep your posts brief. Avoid politics! The same goes for religion and sexual issues. LinkedIn also has job postings and links to job sites. Use them.

Where to Look

Look for job listings you're qualified for. If you've earned a certificate or graduated from a community college or career or traditional college or university, you may get job placement assistance from counselors, teachers, or your advisor there.

To find potential employees, many businesses routinely attend job fairs or career days at these schools, as well as in the community. A job fair is an event for companies with openings to meet potential employees. These are good for entry level job seekers and those with just a little work experience. If one is scheduled at your institution, be sure to attend.

Wear professional clothing and bring copies of your resume. If you have different resumes targeted at different types of jobs, bring them all. Bring business cards with your contact information. You can make your own cards on your computer. Or, you can order some online or at office supply stores, traditional printers, or other places that make copies.

Meet as many of these recruiters as possible. Meet other job seekers, too. You are building a professional network in your industry. Follow up with e-mails or personal notes saying you enjoyed meeting them and are interested in working for their companies.

Representatives of professional IT staffing and recruiting companies can also connect you with jobs in your area. Type "IT staffing" into your Web browser and visit their sites. Many list jobs you may qualify for.

Search the Internet for openings in your city or places you're willing to move to. Several websites are dedicated to helping you find a job. Or enter "job openings information technology" or "job openings and (the specific IT job you're qualified for)" and your city and state into your Web browser.

Ask a Librarian

Local libraries also help job seekers. For example, the Queens Public Library in New York City offers workshops and one-on-one help with resumes, online job applications, interview preparation, job search strategies, and online networking. It

WEBSITES FOR JOB HUNTERS

When you're ready to look for an IT job, search these websites. Many of them specialize in information technology jobs. You can include your ZIP code or city and state in the search box to help you find work in your own community.
- ComputerJobs.com
- JustTechJobs.com
- Indeed.com
- Dice.com
- JobsMonster.com
- CareerBuilder.com
- TheLadders.com
- SimplyHired.com
- USAJobs.gov

ON THE (JOB) HUNT

Libraries often offer programs and resource materials to help in a job search, including resume preparation, interviewing skills, pre-employment practice tests, and access to job listings.

also provides access to several job search databases. The Kansas City, Missouri, Public Library offers employment services through its H&R Block Business & Career Center. Patrons get help conducting online job searches, creating resumes, learning interview tips, and practicing pre-employment tests.

The San Francisco Public Library has a Job Seekers' Lab that offers handouts, books, and staff assistance to patrons. It also holds drop-in events for job seekers. Patrons can attend such classes as "Let Us Amaze You! Useful Tools for Your Job Search," "LinkedIn for Job Search: Beginners Level 1," and "Job Searching with Social Media."

In addition, librarians can help you research businesses you're interested in working for. They can help you find articles and other information about key officials in those companies.

GETTING A JOB IN **THE IT INDUSTRY**

Job help centers and employment offices/services from city, state, and federal governments also stand ready to assist you. The American Job Center Network is a federal program that provides access to federal programs and local resources to help you find a job. It's available online. It also has nearly 3,000 physical locations where you can investigate training programs and job resources throughout the United States.

Narrow your job search to places you'd like to work. Then contact the employers or go online to get and fill out applications.

Attend job fairs to meet employers and other job seekers in the IT industry. Meet as many people as you can. Trade business cards, and stay in touch.

CHAPTER FIVE

Interviewing for IT

Just about the time you think no one will ever hire you, you'll get a phone call or e-mail inviting you to come in for a job interview. A job interview is a conversation between an employer and a potential employee. The employer's goal is to find a new worker. Your goal is to get a job.

If your first contact is by telephone, try to calm any nerves you have. Speak slowly and clearly. And keep a confident tone in your voice. Ask for the name of the person you will talk to. Also ask whether there will be any pre-employment testing. If so, find out what kind it is and where you might find sample tests. Once you set a date and time, your preparation can begin. If pre-interview testing is involved, check online for sample tests you can practice with.

Be Prepared

Find out everything you can about the employer and the person(s) who will interview you. Look for them on Facebook, LinkedIn, Google+, and other social media. Search the company website for stated goals, leaders, and recent news releases. See if you can determine the direction the employer is headed. Then come up with ways you can help them go there. Also search for newspaper and magazine articles about the company and their leadership.

Other social media platforms, including networking site LinkedIn, as well as more casual networks like Facebook and Google+, can help you learn about a potential employers, and may provide info on individuals who will interview you.

Investigate the salary ranges for IT jobs in your area. Get an idea what to expect. You can learn this from your information interviews. You can keep track of salaries offered in descriptions of job openings you see online. You can also check such websites as Salary.com. And don't forget about your school. Counselors there may know how much their graduates earn. Once you have this information, determine three figures. What is the least amount you'll accept? What would be a fair salary that makes you happy? How much would knock you off your chair?

Rehearsal Time

Don't wait until the day of the interview to find the employer's location. Look for directions on GPS, MapQuest, Google Maps, or other places that give driving directions. If you're planning to drive to the interview, drive the route a day or so before the appointment at the same time of day. Notice road work that might slow you down. Plan where you will park. Estimate walking time to the office. If you're using public transit, take a preview trip at the same time and day of the week. Notice how long it takes to get there. Then add an extra ten to fifteen minutes to allow for mini emergencies on the way.

It also helps to practice for your interview beforehand. Look online or in books for typical job interview questions. Think about possible answers before the interview, but don't try to memorize answers. Once you're there, you want to appear spontaneous and genuine, not scripted. Practice with parents or friends.

Your interviewer wants to get a sense of what you're like and how you will fit into the workforce. Be prepared to discuss items on your resume. However, you're likely to be asked about other topics, too.

Dress for Success

The best attire for a job interview in the IT industry is a well-fitting business suit. That goes for both men and women. Even though the employer's dress code may be business casual, you want to make a great impression when you walk in. It's better to be a little too formal than too relaxed.

GETTING A JOB IN **THE IT INDUSTRY**

Several days before your interview, get directions to the site and do a practice run at the same time of day. Pay attention to travel time and any road work or other sources of potential delays.

INTERVIEWING FOR IT

Be sure your hair and fingernails are clean and neat. Women need a manicure in a clear or conservative color. Avoid glitter and wild hues. Cover any tattoos. Remove body piercings that show. (You can leave in your belly button ring.)

Men should carry a briefcase with their resume and any other important papers in a neat folder. For a professional look, women should carry either a purse or briefcase. Not both. And avoid dangling earrings and gaudy or religious jewelry.

Today's the Day

The day of the interview, arrive in the office between five and ten minutes early. Earlier makes you seem too eager—or worse, desperate. Later—well,s late is never a good thing. Turn off your mobile phone before entering the workplace. If there is a receptionist, conduct yourself as a professional while you wait. Many employers use a receptionist as your first interview.

ASKED AND ANSWERED

Practice for your interview with a parent, friend, or trusted adult. You can't predict every question. However, rehearsing will give you a feel for what an interview is like. You'll feel better prepared if you've done a few trial runs. Here are some potential questions you might be asked:

- Why do you want this type of job?
- How can you contribute to this business?
- What types of IT jobs do you like best?
- Tell me about a project you worked on.
- What are your long-term goals in this industry?
- How are you different from other successful IT applicants?
- What are your strengths?
- What are your weaknesses?
- Tell me about a presentation you made on a problem topic.
- What was your biggest mistake on your ABC Project?
- How have you dealt with a coworker who wasn't doing his or her share of the work?

Be ready with brief, simple, and specific answers. Don't memorize answers or practice too much; be easy and natural.

He or she will be asked how you acted when you thought no one was looking.

When you meet your interviewer, repeat his or her name as you make eye contact. Firmly shake hands. Try to relax. Remember at all times that not getting any particular job is not the end of the world. Putting too much pressure on yourself will only backfire on you.

You want to appear confident, but not cocky. Be polite. Wait to be invited to sit. Be friendly. Look for anything personal in the office that you can relate to. If you see a fishing picture, you might mention that you like to fish (if you do). If you see a trophy or award of some kind, ask about it. Try to create a personal connection. Don't waste too much time on trivia, however.

Listening Skills

When the interviewer asks a question, listen carefully. Make eye contact and smile before answering. Ask him or her to explain questions you're not clear about. Many people like to speak and explain things, and interviewers are the same as anyone else.

Keeping your body language "open" is important during an interview. Crossed arms or legs create psychological barriers instead of connections between you and the interviewer.

Be familiar with your resume. Don't look down at it before you answer a question about something on it. Stay accurate (both on the resume and during the interview) about your skills and experience. Your claims will be checked out, either now or during your employment. Inaccuracies can be cause for firing.

During the interview, ask your own questions. Ask about the company based on your research. Let your interviewer know that you took the time to be informed about the employer. Ask about the job. What duties will I perform at first? What opportunities will there be for me to learn more and gain more experience?

Avoid questions about benefits or vacations. That comes after you get an offer. Instead, focus on what you can do for the business. Ask if there will be more interviews (often there will be more than one). Ask when they expect to make a decision.

Most important: Ask for the job. It's unlikely that you'll be hired on the spot. But it doesn't hurt to ask. Stay aware of the time. When the interviewer stands, it's your cue to leave. At the end of the interview, smile and shake hands again.

Show Me the Money

A few days after the interview send an e-mail or handwritten thank you note and again express interest in the job. This polite act is seldom done for jobs in the IT industry, but again, it doesn't hurt. You may or may not be contacted if you don't get the job. So, check back in a few days or weeks via phone or e-mail. Ask about the status of the opening. If the job has been filled, thank the interviewer. Ask to be considered for future openings. Apply elsewhere.

However, if you get a job offer, congratulations! If you like it, you can take it and run. Or, you can negotiate for a better deal. Don't be afraid to ask for more money. The employer will not withdraw the offer just because you'd like higher pay. You can always accept the first offer if they don't agree to your request.

In general, though, no matter how much you're offered, ask for a little more—at least your "makes-you-happy" figure. (In fact, some experts advise job seekers to ask for an amount that even they think is too high.) Remind the employer of

Eye contact and smiles go a long way. Employers look for people who will be pleasant to work with, as well as good at the job.

your education and experience and why you'll be a valued employee.

In addition to salary, consider other benefits. You might get a signing or year-end bonus. Ask how often the company will review your performance (and potentially offer a raise). Twice a year is a common time frame in IT. The company may offer a wide range of such additional benefits as a company car, gasoline allowance, paid sick leave, insurance, profit sharing, personal days off, and vacation. Now is the time to clarify these issues, especially if you have more than one offer to consider. Once you and the employer agree on the terms, ask for the offer in writing.

CHAPTER SIX

The First Day and Beyond

Everyone feels useless the first day on a new job. Don't worry. Your day will be taken up with filling out forms, meeting supervisors and co-workers, and settling in to your work space. Arrive ten to fifteen minutes early. Remember your keycard! Follow the employer's dress code. Smile often. Do your best to show confidence.

As you meet co-workers and supervisors, smile. Make eye contact. Use a firm handshake and repeat the person's name. As soon as you get a chance, write down the names and titles. You'll want to know such policies as whether there are scheduled breaks and lunch time. Some IT companies provide lunch or have a cafeteria on-site. They may prefer you eat there rather than leave the building.

Paperwork

Your first day on the job will make you feel like you're signing your life away. The company's human resources department will have many forms for you to fill out and sign. Here are some:

- **Form W-4**. If this is your first job, you may not have considered the amount of federal, state, or city income taxes you're responsible for. Form W-4 tells

GETTING A JOB IN **THE IT INDUSTRY**

> Do not let filling out a federal W-4 form intimidate you. It simply helps determine how much is withheld for taxes every pay cycle. Your employer cannot pay you unless your completed form is on file.

your payroll department how much to withhold from your paycheck for this purpose. You want to be sure that you'll have enough to pay your taxes at the end of the year. At the same time, you don't want to lend the government your money by withholding too much. (Some people like to use withholding as a mini savings account and enjoy getting a nice refund in April. However, this is poor financial planning. Instead, withhold less and save or invest the extra.)

- **Direct deposit form.** Most employers offer or require you to receive your pay by direct deposit. Direct deposit is an electronic system that puts your money directly into your bank account. You'll be asked for your financial institution and account number. This information will remain confidential.
- **Keycard.** Many employers are concerned with security issues. Information technology companies, in particular, have locked access to their offices. In addition to the physical safety of their employees, these companies must protect vital, often confidential, information. A keycard is your access to the building, department, or personal office. Keycards belong to the employer and must be surrendered when you leave the job.
- **Insurance coverage.** Several types of insurance plans may be included in your employer's benefit package. The company may pay some or all of the premiums. Or, you may be expected to cover a portion of them. Possible choices include health, dental, vision, accidental death, and life insurance. In choosing health coverage, be sure to consider the cost of premiums, the amount of deductible (the part you pay before the insurance kicks in), the co-pay, and whether you can see any health care provider or only one in the plan's network. For the other categories, determine whether you will need a plan. For instance, if you have no dependents, you probably don't need life insurance beyond a simple burial policy.
- **401(k) options.** A 401(k) is an employer-sponsored retirement savings plan that remains tax free until

GETTING A JOB IN **THE IT INDUSTRY**

Employers in the IT field are sensitive to security, both for their employees' safety and the digital information they handle. Your keycard lets you access the workplace, while keeping out unauthorized people.

money is taken out of the account. It makes sense to start your retirement saving as soon as possible, especially if your employer matches your deposits into their 401K plan. However, if you have credit card balances or student loan, personal loan, or car loan debt, pay them off before investing. You should also build an emergency fund of three to six months of expenses before paying into a retirement plan.

Getting and Staying There

Your path toward advancement in the IT industry includes experience through projects you work on. The more skills you add, the more valuable you are to your current (and future) employers. You can also take additional college courses toward a higher degree, either through campus classes or online. Or, take more training offered by technology companies. In general, continue your education every way you can.

WHAT TO DO WITH YOUR PAYCHECK

According to Dave Ramsey, financial expert and best-selling author of *Smart Money Smart Kids* and other books, a good budget gives a job to every dollar you bring home. You can only spend it once. So, be sure you have enough to go around.

Here's a sample breakdown. The "other" category includes such items as clothing, mobile phone, entertainment, and gifts.

Housing and utilities	31 percent
Transportation	20 percent
Food	15 percent
Insurance	7 percent
Saving/Investing	10 percent
Other	18 percent

First use the "saving/investing" category to build an emergency fund of $1,000. Use it only for emergencies. (Going to an Adele concert is not an emergency.) After that, use the money in that category to pay off any debts, including credit cards, student loans, car loans, and personal loans. Once you are debt-free, increase your emergency fund to three to six months of expenses. Only then should you consider investing. At that point, a good rule of thumb is to place fifteen percent of your income into a retirement fund through your work or on your own.

Finding a mentor to advise you and give you feedback can help you navigate workplace politics, make valuable connections, and choose the right career moves.

Finding a Professional Mentor

Soon after starting work, look for one or more mentors. A mentor is someone with experience who agrees to help and advise someone with less experience. The mentor shares knowledge, expertise, and professional contacts. He or she can help you:

- develop your skills,
- understand the ins and outs of the IT industry,

- guide you through office politics, and
- introduce you to key people in the IT industry.

You'll benefit from a number of mentors to guide your career. A good way to find a mentor is to join and participate in professional organizations. Look for ones with local chapter meetings and programs. They'll give you chances to meet other professionals in person. Another place to look is LinkedIn.

Once you've identified a potential advisor, contact him or her. Ask to meet in person or by phone. Discuss the possibility of a mentoring relationship. Remember, you are looking for someone to help you as your career advances. Be sure you have the right personal chemistry together. A mentorship doesn't have to be a formal, meet-once-a-month arrangement. It can simply be with someone who encourages you and gives you constructive feedback.

Acing Your Review

Typical IT companies conduct semi-annual reviews. A review is a discussion of your work performance. It's tied to the chance for a pay raise. Before the meeting, list your accomplishments during the review period. (Note: Being on time and doing the job are not "accomplishments.") Be specific about your part in successful projects and how you helped solve issues that arose during them.

Also list your personal goals for the next review period. Include ways you will build on what you've learned. What will you do to improve your value to the employer? As you embark on the rest of your career, do your best on every task. You'll soon advance to jobs with more responsibilities and higher pay.

GLOSSARY

401(k) An employer-sponsored retirement savings plan that remains tax free until money is taken out of the account.

accreditation A voluntary, peer-review practice by a non-government agency that sets standards of educational quality for postsecondary programs.

application A computer software program with a specific use.

binary number system Also known as Base 2, a system where numeric values are represented using only the digits zero and one.

Computer architecture A plan that shows the way software and hardware technology work together to form a computer system.

computer code An arrangement of instructions to a computer where letters and numbers are represented as binary numbers.

computer network A group of computer systems and other hardware devices.

computer system Computers that are connected and share a central storage system, as well as such hardware devices as printers, scanners, or routers.

direct deposit An electronic system that lets an employer deposit payroll checks and other payments directly into an employee's bank account.

hashtag A word or phrase that follows a hash mark (#). It is used to make it easy for those searching for the topic or keyword to find your tweet.

input The data entered into a computer.

interface Computer hardware or software that communicates with other devices and/or programs.

GLOSSARY

information interview A conversation with a professional to learn about an industry and local job market.

internship A temporary work experience that offers on-the-job training.

job fair An event for companies with openings to fill to meet potential employees. Also called a career fair.

job interview A conversation between an employer and a potential employee.

mentor A person with experience who guides, helps, and advises a less-experienced person.

output The result after a computer program performs its tasks.

resume A document that summarizes your education, professional qualifications, and personal and professional experience.

review A discussion of an employee's work performance tied to the chance for a pay raise.

FOR MORE INFORMATION

Association for Computing Machinery (ACM)
2 Penn Plaza, Suite 701
New York, NY 10121-0701
(212) 869-7440
E-mail: cmhelp@acm.org
Website: http://www.acm.org
ACM provides such resources as a digital library, publications, and conferences that support computing as a science and profession. It offers memberships to students and professionals working in the field.

Canadian Information Processing Society (CIPS)
5090 Explorer Drive, Suite 801
Mississauga, Ontario, Canada L4W 4T9
(905) 602-1370
E-mail: info@cips.ca
Website: http://www.cips.ca
CIPS is Canada's association of information technology professionals. It establishes standards and best practices for its thousands of members across Canada.

Computing Research Association (CRA)
1828 L Street, NW, Suite 800
Washington, DC 20036-4632
(202) 234-2111
E-mail: info@cra.org
Website: http://cra.org
CRA is an association of organizations that deal with computing research, computer science, computer engineering, laboratories, and professional societies, whose purpose is to enhance research and advanced

FOR MORE INFORMATION

education in computing. More than 200 North American organizations belong to CRA.

Information Technology Association of Canada (ITAC)
5090 Explorer Drive, Suite 801
Mississauga, Ontario, Canada L4W 4T9
(905) 602-834
Website: http://itac.ca/about-itac
ITAC provides advocacy, networking, and professional development opportunities to the IT industry in Canada and serves as a link between business and the Canadian government.

The Institute of Electrical and Electronics Engineers (IEEE)
3 Park Avenue, 17th Floor
New York, NY 10016
(212) 419-7900
E-mail: society-info@ieee.org
Website: http://www.ieee.org
IEEE is a worldwide association of such technical professionals as engineers, scientists, computer scientists, software developers, information technology professionals, physicists, medical doctors, and others.

National Center for Women & Information Technology (NCWIT)
University of Colorado
Campus Box 322 UCB
Boulder, CO 80309-0322
(303) 735-6671
E-mail: info@ncwit.org

Website: http://www.ncwit.org The National Center for Women & Information Technology is a non-profit organization that seeks to increase the number of female workers in the fields of computing and technology. More than 600 universities, as well as private companies and government organizations, provide tools and resources for students and women in the workforce.

World Organization of Webmasters (WOW)
P.O. Box 1743
Folsom, CA 95630
(916) 989-2933
E-mail: info@joinwow.org
Website: http://webprofessionals.org
The World Organization of Webmasters, also known as WebProfessionals.org, is a non-profit association that provides education, training, and certification for students, teachers, and professionals who create, manage, or market websites.

Websites

Because of the changing nature of Internet links, Rosen Publishing has developed an online list of websites related to the subject of this book. This site is updated regularly. Please use this link to access this list:

http://www.rosenlinks.com/JOBS/it

FOR FURTHER READING

Alliata, Zorina, Lyubov Berzin; Artem Kharats, and Sachin Agarwa. *Get IT! How to Start a Career in the New Information Technology: Is I.T. Right for You?* Alexandria, VA: Better Karma, 2015.

Alpern, Naomi J., Joey Alpern, and Randy Muller. *IT Career Jump Start.* Indianapolis, IN: Sybex, 2012.

Beshara, Tony. *Powerful Phrases for Successful Interviews.* New York, New York: American Management Association, 2014.

The Chartered Institute for IT, ed. *Women in IT: Inspiring the next generation.* Swindon, UK: BCS, 2014.

Coplin, Bill. *10 Things Employers Want You to Learn in College.* New York, New York: Ten Speed Press, 2012.

DeCarlo, Laura. *Resumes for Dummies.* Hoboken, NJ: John Wiley & Sons Inc., 2015.

Fry, Ron. *101 Great Answers to the Toughest Interview Questions.* Wayne, NJ: Career Press, 2016.

Fry, Ron. *101 Smart Questions to Ask on Your Interview.* Wayne, NJ: Career Press, 2016.

Gibson, Darril. *Effective Help Desk Specialist Skills.* Old Tappan, NJ: Pearson Education Inc.: 2015.

Grensing-Pophal, Lin. *The Everything Resume Book.* Avon, Massachusetts: Adams Media, 2013.

Heitz, Ryan. *Hello Raspberry Pi! Python programming for kids and other beginners.* Shelter Island, NY: Manning Publications, 2015.

Kennedy, Joyce Lain. *Job Interviews for Dummies.* Hoboken, NJ: John Wiley & Sons Inc., 2011.

Marlow, Christie. *Presenting Yourself: Business Manners, Personality, and Etiquette.* Broomall, Pennsylvania: Mason Crest, 2014.

McDowell, Gayle Laakmann. *Cracking the Tech Career: Insider Advice on Landing a Job at Google, Microsoft,*

Apple, or any Top Tech Company. Hoboken, NJ: John Wiley & Sons, 2014.

Moran, Matthew. *Building Your I.T. Career: A Complete Toolkit for a Dynamic Career in Any Economy.* Old Tappan, NJ: Pearson IT Certification, 2013.

Reed, James. *101 Job Interview Questions You'll Never Fear Again.* New York, NY: Plume, 2016.

Reeves, Diane Lindsey and Gail Karlitz. *Career Ideas for Teens in Information Technology.* New York, New York: Ferguson's, 2012.

Regas, Tyler. *Getting an IT Help Desk Job For Dummies.* Hoboken, NJ: John Wiley & Sons Inc., 2015.

Rudd, Colin. *Problem Manager: Careers in IT service management.* Swindon, UK: BCS, 2014.

Ryan, Robin. *60 Seconds & You're Hired.* New York, NY: Penguin, 2016.

Sande, Warren and Carter Sande. *Hello World! Computer Programming for Kids and Other Beginners.* Shelter Island, NY: Manning Publications, 2013.

Sookor, Ramesh, Hugh Ingram, Alison Page, and Tristram Shephard. *Making IT Work 1: Information and Communication Technology.* Oxford, England: Oxford University Press, 2014.

Wilcox, Christine. *Careers in Information Technology.* San Diego, CA: ReferencePoint Press, 2014.

Wright, Daisy. *Tell Stories Get Hired: Innovative Strategies to Land Your Next Job And Advance Your Career.* Brampton, ON, Canada: WCS Publishers, 2014.

Zabloudil, Warren C. *Excellence in IT: Achieving Success in an Information Technology Career* Boca Raton, FL: Universal Publishers, 2014.

BIBLIOGRAPHY

Anderson, Cushing and Gantz, John F. "Climate Change: Cloud's Impact on IT Organizations and Staffing." Microsoft, November, 2012. Retrieved December 30, 2015 (https://news.microsoft.com/download/presskits/learning/docs/idc.pdf).

Augustine, Amanda. "How to Find the Right Mentor to Advance Your Career." The Ladders, 2014. Retrieved December 30, 2015 (http://info.theladders.com/career-advice/five-types-of-mentors-to-advance-your-career).

"Best Technology Jobs." U.S. News and World Report. 2015. Retrieved December 30, 2015 (http://money.usnews.com/careers/best-jobs/rankings/best-technology-jobs).

Bureau of Labor Statistics, U.S. Department of Labor. "Computer Support Specialists.) *Occupational Outlook Handbook, 2014-15 Edition.* Retrieved November 18, 2015 (http://www.bls.gov/ooh/computer-and-information-technology/computer-support-specialists.htm).

Bureau of Labor Statistics, U.S. Department of Labor. "Web Developers." *Occupational Outlook Handbook, 2014-15 Edition*, Retrieved *November 18, 2015 (*http://www.bls.gov/ooh/computer-and-information-technology/web-developers.htm).

"Choosing a Vocational School." Federal Trade Commission. Retrieved January 4, 2016 (http://www.consumer.ftc.gov/articles/0241-choosing-vocational-school).

Criscito, Patricia K. *How to Write Better Resumes and Cover Letters.* Hauppauge, New York: Barron' Educational Services Inc., 2013.

Crosby, Tim. "How Becoming a Video Game Designer Works." How Stuff Works, 2015. Retrieved December

30, 2015 (http://electronics.howstuffworks.com/video-game-designer5.htm).

Csorny, Lauren. "Careers in the growing field of information technology services." *Beyond the Numbers: Employment & Unemployment.* U.S. Bureau of Labor Statistics, April 2013. Retrieved November 21, 2015. (http://www.bls.gov/opub/btn/volume-2/careers-in-growing-field-of-information-technology-services.htm).

The Editors Info TechEmployment (Ed.). *Information Technology Jobs in America.* New York, NY: Partnerships for Community, 2014.

"FAFSA Forms and Filing Tips." Edvisors.com, 2015. Retrieved December 30, 2015 (https://www.edvisors.com/fafsa/forms).

"Finding a Mentor." Idealist Careers. 2014. Retrieved December 30, 2015 (http://idealistcareers.org/finding-a-mentor/).

"Complete Guide to an Online Information Technology Degree." Guide to Online Schools. Retrieved Jan 4, 2016 (http://www.guidetoonlineschools.com/degrees/information-technology).

"How to Become a Video Game Designer." A Digital Dreamer, 2015. Retrieved December 30, 2015 (http://www.adigitaldreamer.com/articles/becomeavideogamedesigner.htm).

Isaacs, Kim. "Resume Tips for Technology Professionals." Monster.com, 2015. Retrieved December 30, 2015 (http://career-advice.monster.com/resumes-cover-letters/resume-writing-tips/Resume-Tips-for-Technology-Pros/article.aspx).

BIBLIOGRAPHY

"Job Interview Tips." Hudson Global, 2015. Retrieved December 30, 2015 (http://au.hudson.com/job-seekers/helpful-tips-career-advice/interview-preparation/interview-tips).

Martin, Carole. "10 Interviewing Rules." Monster.com. Retrieved December 30, 2015 (http://career-advice.monster.com/job-interview/interview-preparation/ten-interviewing-rules/article.aspx).

McDowell Gayle Laakmann. *The Google Resume.* Hoboken, NJ: John Wiley & Sons, 2014.

"Online Web Game Programming Degree Specialization." DeVry University. Retrieved December 30, 2015 (http://www.devry.edu/online-education/online-degree-programs/online-web-game-programming-about.html).

Pappas, Christopher. "10 Study Tips For Online Learners." eLearning Industry. June 10, 2015. Retrieved January 7, 2016 (http://elearningindustry.com/10-study-tips-for-online-learners-getting-the-most-out-of-your-elearning-course).

"Program Planning Guide 2016-2017." Olathe Public School District 233, Olathe Kansas: 2016. Retrieved January 4, 2016 (http://www.olatheschools.com/schools2/programs/high-school/curriculum).

Quast, Lisa. "Finding a Mentor Is Easier than You Think." Forbes, January 6, 2014. Retrieved December 30, 2015 (http://www.forbes.com/sites/lisaquast/2014/01/06/finding-a-mentor-is-easier-than-you-think).

Werber, Cassie. "'Find a Mentor' is Great Career Advice. Why Is it So Hard to Do?" Government Executive, November 19, 2015. Retrieved December 30, 2015 (http://www.govexec.com/excellence/

promising-practices/2015/11/
find-mentor-great-career-advice-why-it-so-hard-
do/123842).

Yate, Martin. *Knock 'em Dead Resumes.* Avon Massachusetts: Adams Media, 2016.

Youshaei, Jon. "12 Surprising Job Interview Tips." *Forbes,* October 20, 2014. (Retrieved December 30, 2015).

INDEX

A

Accreditation Board for Engineering and Technology (ABET), 21
American Job Center Network, 48
animation, 18
Association for Women in Computing (AWC), 41–42
Association of Information Technology Professionals, 41

B

Base 2, 9
Black Data Processing Associates (BDPA), 41–42

C

C++, 10, 18
Cisco, 23, 35
cloud infrastructure, 13
code, 8–9, 10, 28
coders, 8
computer engineering, 9, 12, 17, 23
computer hardward, 11–13, 23, 24
computer network, 12
computer network architects, 6, 11–13
computer research scientists, 13–15
computer science, 7–8, 14, 23, 41
computer support specialists, 6, 12, 13
computer systems administrators, 6, 10, 12, 23
computer systems analysts, 6, 7
Council of Higher Education Accreditation (CHEA), 21

D

data analysis, 17
database administrators, 6, 9–11, 12
database languages, 10
data manipulation, 17
data mining, 17
data warehousing, 17
developers, 6, 7–9, 10, 13, 19
DeVry University, 10, 24
direct deposit form, 61
Dropbox, 25

E

e-communication, 18
employment forms, 59–62

F

Facebook, 49
401(k), 61–62
Free Application for Federal Student Aid (FAFSA), 24–26

77

G

game developers, 10
gaming software, 10
Google+, 42, 49
Google Maps, 51
graphic design, 9, 16, 18

H

H&R Block Business & Career Center, 47

I

information security analysts, 6, 13–15
information systems, 24
input data, 9
insurance, 58, 61, 63
Intel, 35
interface, 10–11
Internet, 9, 15, 16, 25, 42, 46
interviewing, 53–56
    after, 56–58
    possible questions, 54
    preparing for, 49–50
    what to wear, 51–53
IT industry
    degree courses, 23–24
    job rates, 5–6
    job types, 6
    training for, 6, 16–24
ITT Technical Institute, 24

J

Java, 18
J.C. Penney, 43
job hunting, 38–39
    job fairs/career days, 45–46
    joining professional organizations, 41–42
    libraries, 46–48
    social networking, 42–45
    websites for, 46
JobShouts, 44

L

land area networks (LANs), 12
LinkedIn, 42, 43, 45, 47, 49, 65

M

managing expenses, 63
MapQuest, 51
median annual wage, 15
mentor, 64–65
MicroJobs, 44
Microsoft, 23, 35
Microsoft Office, 7, 16, 36

N

network architects, 6, 12–13
network system administrators, 6, 10, 12–13, 23

INDEX

O

Occupational Outlook Handbook, The, 16
online classes, 6, 19, 24, 25
output data, 9

P

Perl, 10
Personal Digital Assistant (PDA), 17
Phoenix, University of, 24
programmers, 7, 8–9
Python, 10

Q

Queens Public Library, 46

R

Ramsey, David, 63
résumés
  importance of, 27
  information to avoid, 36–37
  organization of, 29–36
  style of, 28–29

S

salary.com, 50
San Francisco Public Library, 47
Smart Money Smart Kids, 63
software engineering, 23–24
software testers, 19
systems design industry, 9

T

Target, 43
tech focused high schools, 18–19
TweetMyJobs, 44
TwitJobSearch, 44
Twitter, 43–44

U

U.S. Department of Education (USDE), 21
U.S. Department of Labor, 5
U.S. Department of Labor's Bureau of Labor Statistics, 15, 16

V

video production, 18
Visual Basic, 10

W

W-4, 59–60
Walmart, 43
web design, 9, 16, 18–19
web developer, 9, 19
webmaster, 9
wide area networks (WANs), 12

About the Author

Mary-Lane Kamberg is a professional writer specializing in nonfiction for school-age readers. She is the author of *Working as a Mechanic in Your Community*, *A Career as an Athletic Trainer*, and *Getting a Job in Law Enforcement, Security, and Corrections*. She has also extensively written for *Women in Business* magazine, as well as business magazines in the fields of produce, electronic transactions, veterinary medicine, and the hydroelectric industry.

Photo Credits

Cover, p. 1, (figure) londoneye/E+/Getty Images; cover, p. 1 (background), interior pages, back cover F64/DigitalVision/Getty Images; pp. 5, 64 Erik Isakson/Blend Images/Getty Images; p. 8 Edge Magazine/Future/Getty Images; p. 11 Robin Bartholick/UpperCut Images/Getty Images; pp. 14-15 OJO_Images/Getty Images; p. 17 The Boston Globe/Getty Images; p. 18 kr7sztof/E+/Getty Images; p. 20 Joe Raedle/Getty Images News; p. 22 Photofusion/Universal Images Group/Getty Images; p. 26 Christian Science Monitor/Getty Images; p. 28 Chris Hondros/Getty Images; pp. 33, 50 Justin Sullivan/Getty Images; pp. 34-35 © iStockphoto.com/Sadeugra; p. 36 wavebreakmedia/ Shutterstock.com; p. 39 © samuel wordley/Alamy Stock Photo; pp. 40-41 vgajic/E+/Getty Images; p. 44 © Ilyes Sasi/Alamy Stock Photo; p. 47 Spencer Platt/Getty Images; p. 48 Bloomberg/Getty Images; pp. 52-53 Thomas Imo/Photothek/Getty Images; p. 55 AlbanyPictures/DigitalVision/Getty Images; p. 57 PhotoAlto/Eric Audras/Getty Images; p. 60 Stephen Ehlers/Moment Open/Getty Images; p. 62 PhotoTalk/E+/Getty Images

Designer: Nicole Russo; Editor: Philip Wolny;
Photo Researcher: Philip Wolny

South Hagerstown High School
30380000027989
Kamberg, Mary-Lane
Getting a job in the IT industry
004.023 KAM